Practical Techniques for Building the High School Marching Band

Practical Techniques for Building the High School Marching Band

Starting and Developing the Marching Band Program

K. Owens Davenport, Ed.S.

To order additional copies of this book, contact:
Xlibris Corporation
1-888-795-4274
www.Xlibris.com
Orders@Xlibris.com
53286

Contents

To God be the Glory

I dedicate this book to my wife Veronica. I love you dearly.

Also to my two Princesses, Victoria and Alexandria.

*And to Janice, Tony, David, Mary, Garey, Mark,
Karen and Mother Collins.*

Thank you for supporting me and giving me hope.

Introduction

Marching band has become an integral part of the culture of many schools in today's society. The marching band serves, in many cases, as the ambassador for the school, as well as entertainment during most sporting events. However, the quality of the marching band program, especially in the urban environment, seems to be deteriorating rapidly. Although there are many reasons for this, it can be mainly traced back to the lack of knowledge possessed by the band director. Understand that this is not an attack on those that have chosen to go into our profession. The concern is not normally with those things that we are taught in our theory, history, methods and education courses, it lies with those things that we are **not** taught, but are faced with on a daily basis as a band director.

The purpose of this book is to present those things that a new band director, or a band director that wants to improve, must consider and be ready to confront during the course of the normal operation of a marching band program. This book presents topics in a conversational manner without being a step-by-step instruction guide on how to perform each of these topics. It is written in a way that allows the director to approach each situation with his individual philosophy on how to accomplish things in a way that is most conducive to his program.

This book also gives ideas in some areas that have been proven successful in an urban setting, and can be adjusted for anyone's current program. While these ideas are opinion, they are opinions that have been tried and can work when approached properly.

It is the hope of the author that the information presented here will be helpful to the new director, and accelerates the practical learning curve, thereby allowing a successful start, and hopefully help to build a higher quality program.

Chapter 1

Philosophy and Vision

We each have our own personal reasons for becoming a member of a marching band program when we started. We also have personal reasons for staying with it as long as we have. And of course, there are the very powerful reasons that we decided to make it our profession. Your philosophy for the importance of marching band will be based on your own very personal reasons, and will guide you in how you set up your own band program.

Band has become a very important part of many young people's lives. We know that the experiences that we had while in band are things that developed us into who we are now, and will go with us through the rest of our lives. You want to make sure that you develop a program that will give your students experiences that will be as valuable to them as your experiences were to you. Hopefully, you have had to address this issue in your Music Education courses while in college. If not, it is a good idea to put down on paper what life lessons you got from band, so that you can include it within your philosophy. We are not talking about those things that we learned to recite back in music education philosophy classes, or those philosophies of the great music education theorists, but what you consider important, and what you intend to do for your students.

In any band experience that you have had, you learned something from it. You learned what to do to have an effective program, or you learned what not to do to have an effective program. It is probable that you learned some of each in every situation. So, start with reflecting on each program you have been involved with, ask yourself these questions; 1) What made that program most effective on a daily basis? 2) What could have been changed that would have made that program even more effective? List the attributes that answer each of these questions, and you will begin to see your personal philosophy start to develop. In furthering that philosophy you must add those elements that lead to any great music program, mainly, the teaching of sound musical practices, and developing self-discipline and self-confidence.

You must also decide on the marching band's importance within the whole instrumental music program. Some directors approach marching band as if it is the center of the entire band program. In my opinion, this philosophy will stifle the musical development of your overall program. The marching band must be developed as a part of the overall band program in your school. If you want to develop a musically strong marching band, all students should be a part of a concert band as well. This is where students get to develop fundamental skills that will improve musicianship, and will eventually improve the sound of the marching band. In the following diagram, there is an example including marching as a part of an effective band program:

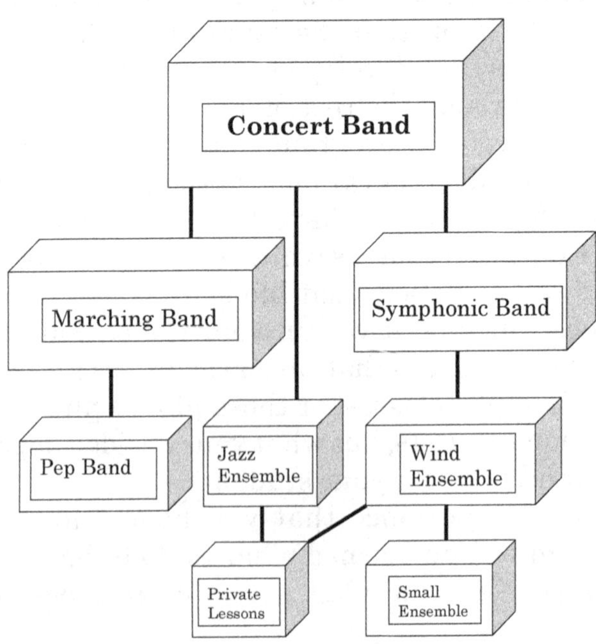

Notice that in this diagram marching band is only a part of the overall band program, and that the entire program becomes an outgrowth of concert band. It is important to notice that this is the diagram of a developed band program, and is something that should be worked towards. In your current situation, you may only have the concert band and marching band elements of your program. That is fine, as long the proper importance is given to each branch of the program. Consider this overall design when developing your philosophy for your marching band program.

Vision

If you decide to take a journey of any kind there are three things that you must know: 1) where you are, 2) where you want to go, and 3) how you are going to get there. So it is with developing a band program. Your philosophy and vision for your program must answer these three questions. Let us discuss each of these things in more detail.

A. *Where you are.*

Unfortunately, most new band directors don't get the opportunity to see the band that they are taking over in action before they get the job. If that were possible, most directors would start off differently. Since this is not possible in most cases, other means must be used to figure out where you are. The first is by talking to administrators, parents, and especially students to find out their perceptions on what the program is currently like. You can inquire about band size, band style, discipline, types of performances that are done, and how the community and school feel about them. This knowledge can give you an idea of what you are facing. Locating pictures and videos can be an extremely valuable asset in finding out where you are. You should try to secure videos of the past band as soon as you get the job. This will give you an immediate idea of what you are dealing with. You can usually find videos by asking students and parents that have been with the band. You may even want to watch some of these videos with students and parents present. Very valuable information tends to come out when students watch videos of themselves. Everything from discipline issues to the morale of the group will be offered freely without you having to ask. These videos give you a chance to evaluate the marching band program in action, and helps you to begin to develop a plan for improvement.

Another good source for gathering information is past score sheets. If the band that you are taking over has participated in marching band competitions in the past, try to locate the score sheets. These score sheets will give you an adjudicator's perspective on what the band does well, and what needs improvement. Take the time to read each of them completely and gather as much information as possible.

B. Where You Want To Go.

The direction that you want to go will be based on different factors. First of all, your philosophy will come into play. A band is a direct reflection of the philosophy of the band director. However, other elements need to be taken into consideration when developing your direction. First, in your interview it is very important that you ask the administrators what elements and types of performances that they find important. You want to make sure that these elements are incorporated into the program in order to maintain support. It is also important to talk to parents and students to discover what they consider important. This will help in maintaining morale and aide in recruitment. Once you have taken all of these things into consideration, you can start to form the *first* vision of the band you want to have. The reason this is the first vision is because as you develop as a director, your vision will be refined.

Your next objective will be to find examples of band programs that have developed in the direction you want your program to go. Try to secure recordings and videos of such programs to use as demonstrations with your own band. And am not saying to copy what you see these bands doing point for point, but use them as a "compass" for the direction you are planning to go. Also, begin very early taking your band to places where they can witness other groups that have been developed in the same direction. You may even want to develop a "sister band" relationship with a group that is more developed than your own, but shares the same basic philosophy.

C. *How You Are Going To Get There.*

This part will take the most effort. While we all have been at least through a series of undergraduate classes that were supposed to prepare us for our profession, in most cases, these classes have barely scratched the surface when it comes to developing a superior marching band. Hopefully, you were fortunate enough to be in a college band that had a director that allowed you to ask questions, and be an active participant in the preparation of band performances. However, even these experiences will only carry you so far. If you want to develop a superior marching band, one thing helps more than anything else—***networking***. If you really want to find out how to organize, rehearse, and direct a superior marching band, it is very important to seek out band directors that have been in the field longer than yourself, and have achieved what you hope to achieve. When any successful director thinks back on his first experiences as a band director, his success was contributed to being surrounded by directors that where willing to share their secrets and experiences with him. It is necessary that you have an open mind and a humble spirit to gain the most from these directors. As long as you keep the right attitude, older directors will share a treasury full of knowledge that will propel you much faster down that path that you are aiming for. Inviting directors to come out to your rehearsals and performances and critique your band is a great way to get direct feedback on what you need to do to improve. When you do this you cannot be thin-skinned. Expect an open and honest response from a director that takes their time to come out and observe, and don't be defensive when the reviews come in.

Another necessary element of learning how to develop your band is attending clinics and workshops. Any director that is serious about his craft, marching or concert band, should attend the Midwest Band and Orchestra Clinic in Chicago. This clinic is attended by thousands of directors and hundreds of vendors. It is an unending source of information for every aspect of a band program. The networking opportunities are endless, and you can always find someone that has a program similar to yours, or has already developed a program with a similar vision as your own. Furthermore, it is an excellent place to start to work on scholarships for your graduates.

In addition to Midwest, you should join your local or regional music association, and attend their regional conferences and workshops. Every opportunity to get exposed to new material will only improve your knowledge and your ability to build your program.

As you talk to directors and get involved in clinics and workshops, you will begin to refine your path, and understand how much is involved in developing a superior program.

Chapter 2

Designing Your Marching Band Program

Now that you have gone through the three steps necessary to define your vision, It is now time to design your marching band program. It is very important to put on paper how your band will be put together. It is a big mistake to go day-to-day with no format on how things will run. Here is a list of questions that you need to answer in order to handle the daily activity of a band program. Answering these questions will put a design in place.

Questions That Effect Design

1. *What style band will I have?*

Since this is a book aimed at show style bands, this one should be easy. However, there are elements within the style that you must decide. One of the main elements is what style of show design will you use? The show designs you may choose from are:

A. Patterns in motion—This design concept moves the band in squads, forming geometric designs and patterns, mainly through pinwheels and step-two's. Many of these design concepts can be found in a series of books entitled *Patterns in Motion* that were put together by Bill Moffitt. Many of the older directors still have copies of these books.

B. Curvilinear—This design concept is basically the same as corps band design, with a show band flavor added to it. The designs are constantly changing, individual movement drills that can be curves or straight line patterns. Some of the best examples of this are found in Drum Corps International performances.
C. Pageantry—This design concept is based on making "pictures" or representations of people or items on the field. These designs can be made through individual or squad movement.
D. Combination—It is possible to combine elements from each of the show concepts to make your own unique blend. It is necessary that you study each drill design style before attempting this.

2. *What standard of knee lift will be required?*

As the band director, you have to decide what standard of knee lift you will require. It can be 90 degrees, 45 degrees, or just get your feet off of the ground. Be sure to use the knee lift that you know how to teach, and that you are willing to enforce. The higher the knee lift, the better physical shape the band must be in. A good practice is to not insist on a marching style that you cannot demonstrate yourself.

3. *What style(s) of music will your band play?*

It is important to expose your band to a variety of musical styles. All top 40 or Hip Hop music limits the musical growth of your students. You should prepare your students to play in the top college bands in the country. These bands play a wide variety of music, including marches, old standard ballads, TV themes, corps style openers, and in some cases, even concert band literature.

4. *How often will you change your show?*

Some bands keep the same show all year. This can lead to extreme boredom in students. Some bands never repeat the same show twice. This never allows the group to perfect a performance. One consideration in how often you change your show has to be whether you plan to participate in field competitions. You need time to perfect a competition show. The important thing is to not change more often than you have time to effectively plan or teach.

5. *How many days per week will the band rehearse?*

This is directly connected with the how often you plan to change your show, and if you plan to participate in competitions. If you don't plan to change your show, then everyday rehearsals will make a boring situation monotonous. You will probably have to adjust the number of days you will rehearse each week, according to what performances are on the horizon, and your desire to perfect your show. The rule of thumb is, if there is nothing in particular that we need to work on, don't rehearse. This keeps the band from burning out, and they are more focused when they are in rehearsal.

6. *How long will rehearsals be?*

This heavily depends on two factors; your endurance and your band's endurance. It does no good to have a three-hour rehearsal if you or the group can only focus for two hours. Another important factor is to not rehearse any longer than what you have planned for. It can be damaging to a program to have students sitting around waiting for you to decide what to do next. Also, it is of extreme importance to learn not to go past your stated ending time. This can get parents very upset and lose their support, as well as lead to students cutting rehearsals to do other things because they can't be sure what time they will get out of rehearsal.

7. *What kinds of performances will your band do?*

Typical performances that you will want to consider are half time shows, competitions, parades, out-of town performances, and community performances. Also make it a habit to take your band to a college homecoming or competition each year. The more we put our students on college campuses, the more they think about going to college.

8. *What kind of student leadership will you develop within the band?*

It is important to get your students involved in the responsibility of keeping the program organized and motivated. There are several different designs for chain of command that can be set up. The most often used design appears on the next page:

Chain of Command

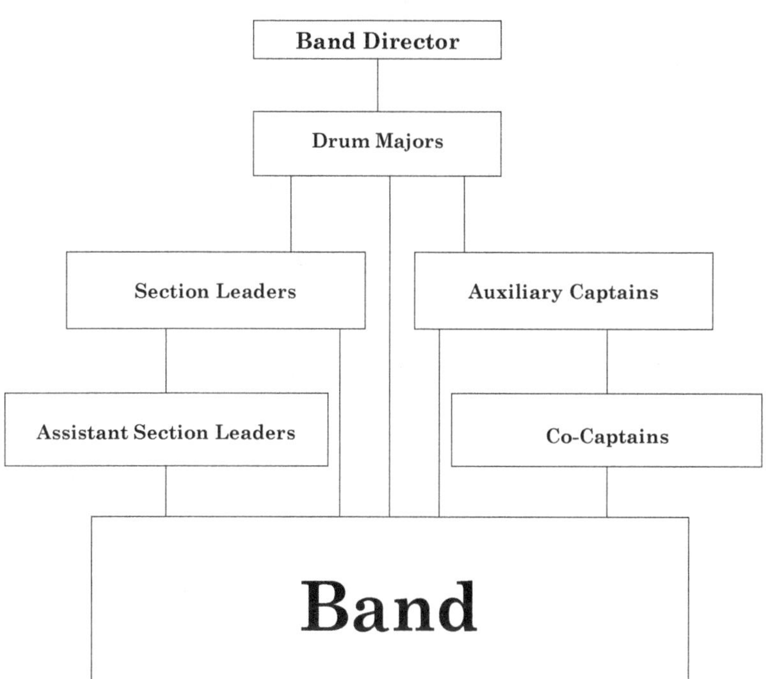

You should assign specific responsibilities for each member of this chain, and hold them responsible for performing their duties, and not overstepping their authority. Also, **keep the responsibility of issuing discipline to a very few people. It is very easy for discipline in the wrong hands to slip into hazing.** There are other kinds of student responsibility groups, such as band officers, military rank systems, etc., but in the beginning you may want to stick with the basics.

9. *What Auxiliary units will you have?*

This is all personal preference. Some of your choices include flags, majorettes (twirlers), dancers, rifle corps, color guard, and banner carriers. The most important thing to keep in mind is only having auxiliary units that you can train or that you have someone that will be responsible for training. Groups of people sitting around with no direction can lead to headaches you don't need. You may want to check with the faculty in your school to see if there are teachers that have participated in auxiliaries, and are willing to serve as a sponsor for your auxiliary groups. If at all possible, avoid using parents of students on these squads as the sponsor of the squad. This can lead to favoritism and a whole different set of problems.

10. *How will you handle disciplinary issues?*

This is a very important issue, and should be thought out carefully. The only pieces of advice that I would give you are 1) be fair with the issuing of discipline, 2) don't have anyone do something that you wouldn't or couldn't do yourself, and 3) use discipline that works towards improving a skill needed in the band. For instance, running a few laps helps to build band members lung capacity, which can lead to better tone production, and build stamina and endurance needed for performances. Be careful that what you use as discipline can be justified in improving the band, and the skills of the individual.

11. *What other musical groups will your students be required to play in?*

It is a good policy to require every player in marching band to participate in a concert band. This will improve musicality in the marching band, and improve reading skills for everyone. You can use other groups within your band program to do the same thing. A student in marching band only will only develop so far as a musician.

12. *Will students be allowed to participate in athletics and be in marching band?*

This can be a very sticky issue. You must rely on your own personal philosophy to make this decision. You may want to consider allowing students to participate in sport that don't conflict with band rehearsal or performances. Eliminating all students that have an interest in sports limits the number of students that you have available for your program. Build a relationship with the coaches in the school, and you may be able to tap into another group of students that could help strengthen your program.

13. *What will be your awards program?*

What awards will be given for completion of each year in the band? What must be achieved to be considered as completing an entire year? What does a student have to do in order to get your recommendation for a scholarship in a college band? Be ready to answer these questions after you have carefully thought them out. This will be discussed later in this book.

Once you have written down your responses to each of these questions, you must internalize the answers and be able to communicate to administrators, parents, and students what your policies will be, and be able to give justification for them.

Chapter 3

The Five Most Important Relationships To Develop Within a School

Upon entering a school, there are certain people that can make your adjustment easier and help you develop your program faster. Seek out each of these people and work on building a cordial relationship with each of these people *before* you are in need of their service. Let's discuss each of these people.

1. **Principal (or administrators)**—In this day of site based management, the principal makes the final decision on many areas that effect your program. The principal makes final decisions on budget, trips, required performances, and **your supplemental salary!** Take the time to sit down with your principal and find out what he or she feels are the important performances and issues concerning the band. Be sure to consider what your principal wants to see in your program. If he or she feels proud of what they are seeing, they will be more supportive of what you want to get done.

   It is very important that you keep your principal informed of all aspects of your program. You do not want information about what you are doing to come from another source. Give copies of all notices that you send to students, parents or the community to you principal before you send them out. Also, make your principal aware of all performances and purchases that you intend to make. Keeping the administration informed in advance will cut down on headaches later on.

2. **Head Building Engineer (custodian supervisor)**— This is an extremely important person to know. This person can get you access to the building, get you the keys that you need quickly, get your room cleaned, and find you whatever furniture that you may need. The building engineer will continue to be of help when you begin to have concerts in the school. However, the most important reason for having a good working relationship with the engineer is **security.** The person that supervises all of the cleaning staff in your building can make sure that someone keeps an eye on your area, checking behind you to make sure the room is secure, and watch for unauthorized people in the area. They can also make sure the most trustworthy people are assigned to clean your room.

   Be sure to communicate with the building engineer any time that you plan to be in the building, particularly during hours that the rest of the building is not in use. It may be necessary for this person to disable alarm systems, as well as secure additional space for sectional or other small group practices. Once again, keeping the lines of communication open will make things run more smoothly for you.

3. **Financial Secretary (school treasurer)**—This person, of course, controls the money matters within the school. There will be occasions when you will need a check written at the last minute, have a bill paid, find out a budget amount, or get moneys collected from students. The financial secretary is responsible for these things. This person can get a check pushed through the principal for you, and in some cases, find some extra money that may be hidden in the budget to help you buy something you really need. Always make sure that you maintain good records on all money that you collect, make sure that it is counted and receipted properly, and turned in on time.

The more that the financial secretary can count on you to complete things properly and on time, the more willing she will be to do things for you when you need them.

4. **Head Guidance Counselor**—One of the hardest struggles for a band director is getting your students signed up for the proper band class. A head counselor that is on your side can help you deal with scheduling issues, and can make sure that band is pushed as a choice when registering incoming ninth graders for the following year. Even more important, this person can get those people removed from your class that should not be there. There are many horror stories about the band class becoming a dumping ground for students that don't have another elective that they can be put in. If the head counselor is on your side this situation will not develop.

   Once again, the most important thing is communication. Before the beginning of the year, write out a course syllabus and prerequisites for each class that you will teach. Immediately let the counselor know of any student that does not have the proper background for the class they are assigned to. Try to work out any conflicts directly with the counselor before going to the principal with your concerns.

   Developing a good relationship with the head counselor serves another important purpose. This person can give you access to the student records of every student in the school. This information can be of considerable help when it comes to recruitment, and will be discussed further in chapter 4.

5. **Athletic Director**—The athletic director generally has control over setting up the sports schedule for the year. This person can keep you informed about upcoming events, as well as extending half-time for some special performances you may like to do. In many schools, practice space is at a premium. There are situations where the band has nowhere to practice. The athletic director can help you to negotiate with coaches for practice field time,

and help to arbitrate in cases where there is a conflict over a student that is a band member and an athlete.

Try to start from the first day that you are in the school to begin developing each of these relationships. Speaking to people each day and sharing your vision for the program when you have the opportunity goes a long way toward getting each on these people on your side, and will help make running your program a little easier.

Chapter 4

Finding Your Personnel

Now that you have a philosophy and a vision, have designed a program, and made your connections within the school, it is time to get a band together. It is important to know several different ways of finding out who was in the band, and who are those people that are potential band members. The earlier in the summer that you can start on this, the better. With an aggressive research and recruitment program, you can build a band much faster than would be expected. Here are several ways to find personnel for your band:

1. *Researching the band roster*

As soon as possible after you have been hired for your job, it is important to find out what students were a part of the band the year before. If you are following an organized band director, hopefully he/she left you a complete band roster that will list each students name, address, phone number, instrument or auxiliary, and classification. If you have been this lucky, you are well ahead of the game. If not, don't worry, there are ways to locate this information.

Another alternative is to look for uniform records. There may be documentation that will show you who wore what uniform, and those forms will give you basic information on all students that were in the band the year before. Use these forms to begin to contact students to find out what they play, what grade they are in, and if they plan to participate in the band the upcoming year. If they say they don't know, don't be discouraged. Invite them to come to an informational meeting to find out what the new direction of the program will be.

If neither of the previous attempts have worked for you (or even if they have,) the next method for finding band members is student records. Go to the guidance department with a pad and pencil and ask for permission to look through student records. Look at the schedule for each student for the past two years, and write down the name, address, phone number, and grade of each person that took band. This is a time-consuming venture, but can give you a thorough idea of who has been in the band in the last few years. Once you have collected this information, get on the phone and call each student, being sure to introduce yourself to their parents on the phone if they are available. While making these calls, be sure to ask each student what instrument they play, so that you can start to get an idea of your instrumentation.

2. *Discovering Hidden Treasures*

At your first meeting with the students, once you have explained your vision for the program, ask the students if they know of others that play band instruments that have not been in the band, or planned to get out of the band. This is particularly effective if the band program has not been very good, and the previous director had a personality that turned students off. If you are excited about your plans for the band, at least at the beginning your students will be too. Challenge each student at that first meeting to go out and recruit one more person into the band. Just think, if this works your band will double in size *immediately*! This does work, and it is amazing how proud students get when they know they have recruited someone into the program. When each of these new recruits come to rehearsal, take the time to introduce yourself and welcome them in. Remember, they are still making up their minds about whether they want to be there. The more comfortable they are made, the more likely they will come back to the next rehearsal. In many cases, students like this turn out to be the most dedicated to the program.

3. *Immediate Recruitment*

Although we have just discussed your students recruiting others to the program, there are other steps that you can take to further recruit new members to your program. Here are some other methods:

A. *The Blanket Form Letter*—Every school at some point in the summer sends out a letter from the principal to every returning student welcoming them to a new school year. Find out when this letter will go out, and seek permission from your principal to include a letter of your own in the same envelope. The letter that you include should introduce yourself, tell something about your background, and give a brief but exciting summary of your vision for the band. If possible, attach a basic information form to be returned to you. This form should basically ask for name, address, phone number, parents' names, instrument, number of years played, and grade level. This form further helps you to develop a data base, and gives you an idea of who has an interest in the band.

B. *The school marquee*—First of all, the marquee is the announcement board that most schools have located outside at the entrance to the the school parking lot. This board is used to post messages about upcoming school events. Get permission from your administrator to post information about a marching band interest meeting and the first marching band rehearsal. This will get basic knowledge out into the community.

C. *Public service radio/television*—Cable companies all have a public access channel that posts information on events in the community. Locate the channel, and you should be able to find out how and when you can send in information to be posted. Radio stations tend to do community service announcements at times during the day. Contact each channel that is popular in the area of your school, and send in your announcement. Be sure to include Your name and the **school** phone number where you can be contacted.

D. *School Web Site*—Get permission to have your information posted on the school web site. Here you can post a more detailed advertisement, including information about you, about your vision, and the date of your information meeting and your first rehearsal. Try to post this information in the band area on the school web site, and at least a link on the home page of the school.

4. Long Term Recruitment

Once you have your immediate recruitment in place, it is time to start considering long term recruitment. This may sound rather soon, but it is never to early to begin to consider the future of your program. As soon as possible, find out what middle schools feed your school. Begin to contact the band directors of these schools. Introduce yourself, what kind of program you plan to build, and offer to be of assistance to the middle school director. This person can be a major recruiter for you in years to come. The middle school band director has as much influence on whether or not a student continues to play in high school as anyone. You may even want to find out if the middle school director wants to help with your marching band. This gives you someone to assist you, and if the middle school director is popular with his/her students, it makes them more comfortable with joining the band when they get there.

Recruitment and retention of students within your band program will be an ongoing concern as long as you are a director. The main requirement for handling this problem is being *proactive*. Always look ahead towards future personnel concerns and start developing a plan ahead of time. If you follow the suggestions made in this section, hopefully finding and keeping personnel will be less of a concern as you build your program.

Chapter 5

Communication

Communication is a major key to the development of a strong band program. The better we communicate with students, parents and administration, the more effective we are able to implement our program. Communication—like planning—can take time, but the time spent preparing communication can add to the success and attendance at events. It is important that communication about events go out well in advance. The more advanced notice that you give students and parents, the higher your attendance rate will be. Here are some methods of communication that will be effective.

The Practice and Performance Calendars

The first communication that the band director will want to send out is a schedule of practices and rehearsals. It is important in this day of busy work and activity schedules that you communicate when you intend to have practices, starting with the summer band camp schedule, and going through the entire marching band season. Take the time as soon as possible to sit down and figure out what your schedule will be. Then put it down on paper in an organized form (like a calendar). Be sure to include rehearsal dates, starting and ending times, and the type of rehearsal that it will be (i.e. Music rehearsal, field rehearsal, dance routine, ect.). Make sure that every student gets two copies of this schedule; one for themselves and one for their parents. It is also a good idea to post a copy of each calendar in the band room as a reminder. As further reinforcement, at the end of each practice verbally go over all upcoming events for the week.

Along with a practice schedule, a performance and events calendar should also be issued. Use the same techniques to put out this information. Both the practice schedule and performance calendar should be issued as early in the summer as possible.

The School Web Site and E-mail

Two very effective ways to communicate information that must make it home to students and parents are the school web site and e-mail As soon as you start your new job inquire about getting access to a section of the school web site that you may post information about the band program, including a schedule of practices and events. You will need to either have a person that is responsible to keep this information current, or you may have to do it yourself.

Along with the web site, when you initially collect information from students and parents, make sure that you ask for e-mail addresses. Bulk e-mails are an extremely quick and effective way to send out information instantly, and is an inexpensive way to accomplish it.

The Band Room Chalkboard

It is a good idea to dedicate a portion of your chalk or dry erase board to post reminders to your band students. Use a different color chalk or marker for this part of the board that will stand out, and train your students as a part of the daily routine to check this area of your board.

The Telephone Tree

A good method of communicating information to your parents quickly is by developing a phone tree. A phone tree is started by forming a telephone committee of parents, starting with selecting a committee chairperson. This committee would take your database of telephone numbers of all of your band members and divide it among themselves. When you have information that you need to communicate with parents, you would call the committee chairperson and tell them what the announcement is. Then that parent will give the information to each person on the committee, who in turn calls everyone on their section of the phone list. This method requires dedicated parents, but works very well once it is in place.

Personal Contact

Even with all of the other methods that we have discussed in this chapter, nothing can replace personal contact. It is very important that you spend time communicating with each parent, giving them updates on the progress of their children. This can be accomplished in several ways. First of all, making yourself available after rehearsals while you are waiting for students to be picked up will allow you time to casually talk to parents and address any concerns that they may have, or that you may have. This method takes advantage of time that is usually spent just waiting around. Another method is time during band parents meetings. Have your Band Parent president set aside time during every meeting for you to address all of the parents to discuss upcoming events, concerns and future plans for the band. In addition to these methods of contact, making telephone calls is an important way of communication. You may want to make a habit of contacting five to ten parents a week, just to let them know how there child is progressing.

Taking time to communicate with parents and students in a timely manner will make everything that you do in your program more effective, and eliminate confusion about expectations within your program.

Chapter 6

Forming a Band Parent's Organization

A supportive group of parents can be an invaluable asset to a band director. However, it is important to make sure that this group is organized and has a clearly defined set of goals to work towards. Some of the purposes for a Band Parent's organization are:

1. To support the vision that is set forth by the band director for the band program.
2. To assist the band director with administrative and logistical support as needed.
3. To serve as positive public relations between the band and the community.
4. To aid in raising funds for the band program.
5. To provide moral support and a sense of cooperative involvement between parents and students.

It is important that you understand that the main idea in all these is **support** and not **control.** It is very important that parents do not assume that they are in a position to control what the band does. That is why it is very important that the band director sets goals, purposes and responsibilities for the organization.

As band director, it is your responsibility to clearly communicate with the organization. You must be able to explain your philosophy and goals for the band program. You then must be able to explain how the band parents fit in to accomplishing these goals.

Organizing a Band Parent's Organization

It is important to start a parent's organization very soon after starting your job. The earlier that you get parental support and have them share your vision, the easier it will be to establish your program. The following steps should be followed in order to start the parent's organization:

1. **Ask the principal if a parents' organization is already in existence.**

   If there is an organization in place, the principal will probably know who the band parent president is. Contact this person, and set up a time to sit down with them and discuss how the group has been run in the past, how you would like it to operate, and what your vision is for the program. It is important that this person, who is the recognized leader of the organization, understands what you expect from them and the organization. *Be sure you know what you expect before meeting with them!!!*

2. **Use your list of band students as a contact list for band parents.**

   Use the list that you have collected from the various sources that we discussed in chapter four to contact parents about the first meeting. It would be a good idea to already have a date set for the band parent's meeting before contacting students for the first band rehearsal. This way you can use the same contact to announce both events.

3. **Find a venue to have your first meeting.**

   This may sound simple, but carefully think this through. You will want the place that you have the first meeting to be large enough to hold all of the parents comfortably. You also want to make sure that the room has good enough acoustics that you can be clearly heard by all parents in the room. A room too large may make it hard for parents in the back to hear. You also want a room that will allow you and the parents to be able to meet uninterrupted. Having a parents meeting in the band room immediately after a band practice could lead to a lot of distractions from student noise. Make sure that the room is clean and orderly. Remember, this will be the first impression that many of the parents will have of you. They will judge you by the atmosphere you bring them into.

4. **Practice what you will say to them.**

If you are not comfortable talking in front of people, use your friends and family to practice on. You want to show confidence in what you are trying to communicate with the parents. Start well in advance putting your ideas together, and then practice what you are going to say. It may even be of help to have someone play "devil's advocate". Have them ask you uncomfortable or difficult questions to get you used to responding comfortably.

5. **Have a list of things that you would like the parent's organization to start working on.**

At that first meeting, once you have discussed your philosophy, vision, and structure of the band program, have a list of projects that you want the parents to address right away. It is important that the group has things to immediately start organizing. Some of these things can be organizing uniforms, organizing a concession stand, organizing a fund-raiser, preparing for a trip or performance, or many other ideas. Always have this group working on something. Otherwise, they will start to concentrate on things they want you to change!

The Band Parent Constitution

The first thing that you must put in place when organizing a band parent's organization is a constitution. The constitution puts in place the way the band parent's organization will be run. The next several pages will give you an example of a band parent constitution:

Constitution
School X High School
Band Parent's Association

Article I

The name of this organization shall be the School X High School Band Parents Organization.

Article II

Purpose

The purpose of this organization is to assist the Band Director; to help raise funds for financial assistance for the band through the operation of the concession stand and special projects; to provide spiritual support; and to provide chaperones for parades and all other band related events.

Article III

Membership

Membership shall consist of parents and guardians of active School X High School Band students and honorary members.

Article IV

Officers

The officers of this organization shall include:

President
1st Vice President
2nd Vice President

Recording Secretary
Corresponding Secretary
Treasurer
Assistant Treasurer
Parliamentarian
Chaplain
Historian

Article V

Meetings

Meetings shall be held as stated in the bylaws.

Article VI

Amendments

This constitution may be amended by a majority vote of active members present and voting at any regular meeting. Notice of the proposed amendments must be submitted at the previous regular business meeting of the organization. All such proposed amendments shall be submitted in writing and signed by two active members.

Bylaws

Article I

Membership

Section I   Membership shall consist of parents and guardians of active School X High School Band students. Only parents and guardians of current active band students may hold office in the association.

Section II   Honorary members shall consist of members who show interest in the welfare of the School X High

School Band. Honorary members may not hold an office or be a committee chairperson.

Section III — When there is but one candidate for office, the election by ballot may be dispensed with and the election shall proceed by acclamation.

Section IV — Election will be held in April of each school year.

Section V — Installation of officers shall take place in May of each school year. The newly installed officers shall assume office June 30th and hold office until June 29th of the next year.

Section VI — The retiring officers shall surrender to their successor all materials pertaining to the business of the School X High School Band Parent's Association by June 30th.

Section VII — Officers shall be elected for one year and may hold an office for no more than two consecutive terms.

Article II

Absenteeism

Section I — Any officer or committee chairman who accumulates more than three unexcused absences from meetings will be asked by the executive Board to resign and someone else will be appointed by the President to serve out the unexpired term.

Section II — An officer or committee chairman excused from a meeting is expected to send to that meeting a written report of any information due at that time.

Section III — Exceptions shall be made in emergencies.

Article III

Duties of Officers

Section I   The President shall preside at all meetings of the Association. He/she shall ensure that the books of the Treasurer are audited as provided in the Bylaws. The President, with the approval of the Executive Board, shall fill vacancies occurring while in office. He/she shall appoint committees not otherwise provided for according to *Robert's Rules of Order, Revised.* The President shall also serve as Chairman of the Executive Board.

Section II   The 1st Vice President is responsible for ways and means (finances). The 1st Vice President shall also preside over meeting in the absence of the President.

Section III   The 2nd Vice President shall be responsible for concessions.

Section IV   The recording Secretary shall keep a full and correct account of the records and minutes of each meeting, and shall keep a record of the Treasurer's report and all committee reports. The Recording Secretary shall also issue a copy of all minutes to the Band Director and to the Principal.

Section V   The Corresponding Secretary shall attend to all correspondence and keep a record of same, shall purchase all secretarial supplies, and shall keep an accurate account of the names and addresses of all members, including honorary members of the Association.

Section VI   The Treasurer shall keep a record of all moneys and make a written financial report at each monthly meeting. He/she shall expend no money unless approved by the Executive Board. The Treasurer shall deposit all money into the Association's account by the end of the next school day. The Treasurer shall maintain copies of all purchase orders drawn from the fund.

Section VII   The Assistant Treasurer shall assist the Treasurer with all monetary transactions and record keeping.

Section VIII   The Parliamentarian shall, when necessary, advise the President on proper procedures for conducting meetings according to *Roger's Rules of Order, Revised.*

Section IX   The chaplain shall provide spiritual guidance and leadership within the Association. The Chaplain shall open all meetings with prayer.

Section X   The Historian shall maintain a scrapbook of all activities and events of the band and the Association held during the year.

Article IV

Standing Committees

Section I   The President, with the concurrence of the Executive Board, shall appoint all committees as deemed necessary. Some of these committees are Chaperone, Uniform, Awards, Ways and Means, and Public Relations.

Article V

Executive Board

Section I   The Executive Board shall consist of the Band Director, President, 1st Vice President, 2nd Vice

President, Recording Secretary, Corresponding Secretary, Treasurer, Assistant Treasurer, Parliamentarian, Historian, and chairpersons of all committees.

Article VI

Finances

Section I The President and the Executive Board, with the Band Director, shall prepare a proposed budget of the Association that shall be presented to the voting body at the August meeting of the Association for approval and adoption.

Section II The budget shall be based on the previous year's income and expenditures, and new projects assigned by the Band Director.

Section III Any officer or committee handling Association funds shall, as a matter of record, give the Treasurer a full written account of expenditures and funds collected, and shall also make a full report to the Association.

Article VII

Meetings

Section I The regular monthly meeting of the School X High School Band Parents' Association shall be held on the first Wednesday of each month.

Section II The Executive Board shall hold its regular monthly meeting on the fourth Wednesday of each month.

Section III The President may call a special meeting of the Association if two (2) members of the Executive Board or the Band Director request a meeting.

Article VIII

Amendments To The Constitution

Section I   Procedures for amending the Constitution or establishing Bylaws shall be as follows:

1. The President shall appoint a committee to develop any constitutional changes.
2. A copy of the proposed change shall be presented and read at a regular meeting of the Association.
3. At the next regular meeting, a majority vote to the affirmative of the membership in attendance is required for adoption of the change.
4. All changes to the Constitution must be approved by the Band Director and the Principal.

While a constitution lays an outline for how the band parents' organization should operate, it is important that the band director continue to give focus to the organization. Make sure that you work fairly with all parents. It is dangerously easy for factions to develop within a parents organization, and power struggles can occur. Continue to emphasize that all are there for the same reason: to support **ALL** of the band students.

Be sure that you have a system to thank those parents that spend their time helping the band. Dedicated parents that you can trust to handle certain tasks for you can make your job a whole lot easier. Within your awards system, have a plan to reward hard working parents. You will find that the same set of parents will be the ones that do most of the work.

Utilize your parents organization to its full potential. A properly organized and running parents group can take alot of the work and pressure off of you, and will be a benefit in retaining students in your program. If a student's parents are active, the student will probably remain active, and will not be a discipline problem if they know mom and dad will be around as well. Let those parents that give their time to help the program know that you appreciate them, and they will support what you are doing long after their child graduates.

Chapter 7

Maintaining and Purchasing Instruments

The instrumental inventory at your school will be the most expensive responsibility you will have as a band director. Most instrument inventories run into the hundreds of thousands of dollars. Although you may not be told this directly, *you are financially responsible for that inventory once you become the band director!*

Your principal just shook your hand, said congratulations, and handed you your keys. What is the first order of business you must take care of? **Check your inventory!!!** It is extremely important that you immediately check to see what is there the day you take over so that you will not be held responsible for things that have disappeared before you got there. There are two ways that you can accomplish this:

The School / Band Inventory List

If you are coming into a program that has been organized for awhile, there is a good chance that a printed inventory list exists. Ask your principal if an inventory list is available, and if it is, secure a copy immediately. Once you have this list in your hand, immediately check what is on this list against what is in the band room. This can be time consuming, but if at all possible **do a hands-on assessment *yourself*.** Doing it yourself lets you know for sure what is in the band room and what you are responsible for, because you have seen each item with your own eyes. You also get an idea of what condition your instruments are in, so that if you need equipment repaired or replaced before practices start, you have time to address the situation. Once you have checked your inventory against the list, report *in writing* any discrepancies to your principal immediately. It may be even more advantageous to have him sign a copy of the discrepancy report, then you file it where you can always get your hands on it. This will protect you against claims of missing equipment while you are director.

Make Your Own List

If you are not able to locate an inventory list in the school, it will be necessary to make your own. This can be time consuming, but it is extremely important that you take the time to do this right at the beginning. Start by going through your instrument storage areas and band room and record every instrument that is there. You want to record the kind of instrument, the make, the model (if known), the serial number, and the condition. Once you have collected this information, create a database for yourself, leaving room to record what student checks it out during the school year. Once you have completed the database, print out a copy for your files (it is important to store a hard copy), then give a copy to your principal, your department chair, and the financial secretary. You want to give it to multiple people so you have multiple sources just in case you need to find it. Make sure that you get your principal to sign your hard copy.

If you are still in college, or have not started your job but have access to a band room, you can save yourself some time by locating where Serial numbers are located on the different instruments. Give yourself the assignment of listing each instrument in the band, and the location of serial number. Keep this info in a portfolio, so that when you get on the job you can refer to it.

Instrument Repair

Once you have checked your inventory, you will more than likely run into instruments that must be repaired. Repair of instruments can be an extremely expensive venture. However, there are ways to bring down the price tag on these repairs. It is important to understand that most of the money spent on instrument repair is spent on labor. You can significantly reduce the amount of money spent by doing the following:

1. *Buy a high quality tool kit*—Purchase a kit that will allow you to handle the simple maintenance items that come up during the year. Things such as oiling valves, pulling and greasing slides, and replacing corks are things that can be done by you, and waste money when sent to a repair shop. Three or four repairs done by you will more than pay for the tool kit. If you have no experience maintaining instruments, buy a how—to book for simple maintenance items.

2. *Know exactly what is wrong with an instrument before you send it out*—You can waste money by sending instruments out and simply saying "put it in playing condition. Understand that repair shops are in business to make money. The time that it takes for the shop to investigate each instrument to discover what is wrong is money out of your budget. If you are a brass player, you should be able to figure out what needs to be repaired and add a note in the case stating what needs to be done. If you are a woodwind player, the same thing applies. See if you can find another teacher that plays instruments that you don't feel comfortable play testing to check those instruments.

3. *Get repair quotes before approving repairs*—It is actually possible to spend more to repair an instrument than it costs to replace it. Don't send out instruments that look like puzzle pieces to be put back together useless absolutely necessary. This wastes a lot of the repair shop's time, and a lot of your money. And chances are you will be sending it out again.

4. *Start a repair log on instruments that go out for repair*—Document each instrument that you send out for repair. Keep a check of whether the same instrument continues to have to be repaired. Instruments can suffer

from metal fatigue or metal thinning. If you find an instrument that is continually going to the shop, take it out of service. Replacing this instrument will be more cost effective.

The bottom line when it comes to this topic is *know your equipment*. Don't waste money on things that you can do yourself. The more money that you can save on repairs, the more you have available for purchasing new instruments. Above all, develop a sense of pride among your students so that they take care of the instruments provided by the school. Have regular inspections, and hold students accountable for broken equipment. Doing this will substantially reduce your repair bill.

Purchasing New Instruments

In most cases, band directors work on a rather small budget. Therefore, it is important when buying instruments that care is taken to make sure that all purchases are cost effective. A series of things should be considered when buying instruments while trying to stay within a budget:

1. *Set priorities based on present and future instrumentation.*
   If you know what your instrumentation will be, and your inventory does not have enough of a certain instrument to ensure that everyone has one, buying additional instruments of that kind is a priority. Sounds simple, but if this is not thought out properly, it is possible to spend money on a wish list instead of a need list.

2. *Shop for economical buys based on quality of instruments instead of brand names.*
   While we would all like to have the top brand names on all of our instruments, there are some very good brands that you may not have much experience with. Some instruments brands that you want to know if you are on a budget, but want quality equipment are Jupiter, Blessing, and Dynasty. Many universities are using marching brass from each of these companies, and the equipment holds up

very well. Most companies have a demo program, that will allow you to play test instruments before buying. Check with your local store to find out how to do this.

3. *Check several sources for prices on instruments.*

    Many school systems require bids when buying equipment over a certain price. Even if it is not mandatory, this is a good practice. There can be hundreds of dollars difference from one store to another on the same instrument. Take the time to shop around. One store that is a must on any bid list is Chuck Levin's Washington Music Center in Wheaton, Maryland. Be sure to check catalogs, web sites, and directories to find the stores that will best serve you.

4. *Only buy instruments that are a necessity to your program.*

    It is wasteful to buy equipment that no one is likely to play. I recently did inventory in a band room that had about $15,000 worth of instruments that had never been used, and most likely would never be used. A previous director had purchased 6 Herald trumpets, and 6 screw-on bell Eb Mellophones, not to mention various other instruments that were still in the cases. These instruments are a result of poor planning. Also, try to stay away from spending money on common instruments that students normally own. Instruments such as flutes, clarinets, saxophones, and trumpets are generally owned by students. While it may look good to have all of the same kind of instrument within a section, and may even have intonation benefits as, if you are working with a limited budget this is not a priority.

5. *Be sure within your plans for buying new instruments, that you include instruments that must be replaced.*

    Buying additional instruments is great, but if the current instruments are of poor quality, replacement of those also become a priority. This, of course, goes back to knowing your inventory.

6. *Learn about "Demo Return" instrument purchases.*

Haven't heard of this? Don't worry, you are not alone. "Demo Return" are instruments that have been play tested by a person and returned to the company. Once the instrument is returned, it can no longer be sold as new. Sometimes as much as several hundred dollars can be taken off of the price for an instrument that is just like new. If you don't ask specifically for Demo return, it will never be mentioned to you. Check with your instrument dealer about opportunities to buy this type of instrument.

7. *Check pawn shops for bargains on good equipment.*

It is amazing what can be found in a pawn shop! You can find everything from marching bass drums to sousaphones. The great thing about pawn shops is that you can negotiate with them and really get a great deal on instruments with a lot of use left in them. Locate your local pawn shops and introduce yourself to the people there and let them know what kind of instruments you may be looking for. There is another reason that you want to keep an eye on your local pawn shops; many times when instruments have been stolen from a school, they will end up there.

In conclusion, it is important when working on a limited budget to stretch your money as far as possible. If you consider each of these factors, your budget will stretch much further, and will help you get the equipment that you need.

Chapter 8

Student Motivation

Student motivation is the single most important factor when trying to build and maintain a band program. If students have personal motives and goals for being in the band program, and feel that they have the possibility of achieving these goals, the chance of students remaining in the program is very high. Personal motivation can be anything from something as small as receiving a varsity letter, to something as big as getting a full scholarship to college. As a band director, it is your job to put reachable objectives in front of your student to retain them.

College Scholarships

As freshmen enter the band program, always stress to the band students and band parents the possibility of receiving college scholarships for playing in the band. Many directors owe their college education to having a band scholarship. It is important to stress to students and parents that it is not necessary to be a music major to receive a scholarship, just to play in the program. Several things can help with using scholarships as motivation:

1. Have a bulletin board in your band room that has band scholarship information at all times. Make sure that these scholarship requirements state that the high school band director's recommendation is a must.

2. Invite college directors to your rehearsals to speak to your students. When they come, have your underclassmen speak to these directors, as well as your seniors. Having 9th and 10th graders speak to college band directors helps to keep them motivated in your program, and gives them a reason to focus on band.

3. Keep a list posted in your band room of students that have graduated and received band scholarships. Be sure to list the name of the student, what they play, and where they went to school. This list proves your point that it is possible to receive a scholarship.

4. Take your band to as many college campuses to perform as possible. Once again, this keeps your students focused on college, and gives them a chance to be exposed to different colleges and different college bands. **Don't just take your student's to your Alma Mater!!!** Although you may have enjoyed your college band experience, it will not meet the tastes of all of your students.

Once you have put the college band scholarship in place as motivation for your students, you become the agent for each of them. As you have students reach their senior year, you should prepare a list of your seniors that contains each persons name, address, phone number, instrument, GPA, SAT or ACT scores, and where you would rate them. The "five star" rating system is a good way to rate them. At the beginning of each year, mail a list to each college that you have students interested in attending, as well as those schools that you know are looking for good students to give scholarships to. Doing this allows college directors to start to contact them early, and brings excitement into those students that have been motivated by the possibility of receiving a scholarship.

The Band Awards Program

One of the strongest methods of establishing student motivation is setting up a consistent awards program. A good awards program is one that establishes awards for years of service in the band, special awards for leadership positions, and special awards for extraordinary achievement.

Awards give students something to shoot for each year. They do not have to be large or expensive things. They simply have to be things that can only be received by reaching milestones within your marching band program. A sample awards program would look like this:

Marching Band Awards Program

Awards for Completing:

First Year Marching Band ....A customized certificate

Second Year Marching Band....An 8" Chenille Varsity Letter

Third Year Marching Band ......A pin-on medal (to be worn on band uniforms during the fourth year)

Fourth Year Marching Band....A trophy (every student that completes 4 years **should** receive a trophy)

Special Leadership Awards

Section Leader Awards .... Plaque

Auxiliary Captains Awards .... Plaque

Drum Major Award .... Trophy

Band Superlative Awards
Most Outstanding Freshman......... Trophy
Most Outstanding Musician........... Trophy
Most Outstanding Marcher............ Trophy
Most Dedicated Bandsman .... Trophy

Many other awards can be added depending on your situation. Also, the Band superlative awards can be voted on by the members of the band, but make sure YOU are the one that counts the ballots. Make sure your band has confidence that the voting is fair.

You will be amazed to find that members of your band that had considered quitting to do other things will remain in your marching band to receive their awards. This is particularly true with rising seniors. They have reached an age where they must decide between band, trying other activities after school, or getting a job. After spending three years in marching band, the knowledge that they will receive a trophy for remaining the last year (especially a nice trophy) will keep them motivated. The important thing that you must do is stick to the requirements that you set to receive each award.

The Band Rank Program

The Band Rank Program is an idea that has been around for a long time. This system is set up to recognize individual achievement by marching band members, both in band activities and in academics. This program rewards those students that fulfill their responsibilities to the band as well as to their academics. It is aligned with a military rank system, and students receive more privileges within the band as they achieve rank. Some of the privileges you may want to consider giving are things such as allowing students to get on buses going to local events from highest rank to lowest rank, or signing the bus list to go on longer trips by rank. It also is a good idea to allow higher rank students to assist you in small decisions that you must make, such as what music to play in the stands, or what music to use in a dance routine. When other students see that these students get these privileges because of higher rank, it motivates them to do those things that will lead to promotions. The following is a sample set of the requirements to receive rank within the marching band:

BAND RANK PROMOTION REQUIREMENTS
*****It is the responsibility of the member to request a promotion at the end of each grading period.**
Forms will be made available. ***

BUCK PRIVATE—Lowest rank; entrance level

PRIVATE—must have gone through the three levels or must have been in the marching band for two grading periods.

PRIVATE FIRST CLASS—must have participated in at least 95% of rehearsals and all performances in a grading period. Must also maintain a 2.0 during that period.

CORPORAL—must meet all requirements for Private First Class, plus maintained a 2.3 G.P.A. Must know all music.

STAFF SERGEANT—participated in 95% of rehearsals and all performances for a grading period. Must also maintain a 2.5 during the same period.

DRILL SERGEANT—participated in 95% of rehearsals and all performances for a grading period. Must also maintain a 2.6 during the same period.

MASTER SERGEANT—participated in 95% of rehearsals and all performances for a grading period. Must also maintain a 2.8 during the same period.

SECOND LIEUTENANT—participated in 100% of rehearsals and 100% of performances for two grading periods. Must have auditioned for All-County Band within the last twelve months. Must maintain a 3.0 during the same period.

FIRST LIEUTENANT—participated in 100% of rehearsals and 100% of performances for two grading periods. Must have auditioned for All-County Band within the last twelve months. Must maintain a 3.2 during the same period.

CAPTAIN—participated in 100% of rehearsals and 100% of performances for three grading periods. Must have auditioned and made All-County Band, or scored at least a 70 in auditions within the last twelve months. Must maintain a 3.2 during the same period.

MAJOR—participated in 100% of rehearsals and 100% of performances for one year. Must have auditioned and made All-County Band, or scored at least an 80 in auditions within the last twelve months. Must hold first chair in symphonic band. Must maintain a 3.4 during the same period.

COLONEL—participated in 100% of rehearsals and 100% of performances for Two years. Must have auditioned and made first-chair All-County Band, or scored at least a 90 in auditions within the last twelve months. Must hold first chair in symphonic band. Must maintain a 3.6 during the same period.

GENERAL—participated in 100% of rehearsals and 100% of performances for Three years. Must have auditioned and made first chair All-County Band, or scored at least 90 in auditions within the last twelve months. Must hold first chair in symphonic band. Must maintain a 3.8 during the same period.

The most important part of establishing this program is to be consistent. Have an established way to pass out forms, evaluate band members, and post promotions at the end of every grading period. Notice that these promotions tie in other aspects of a **complete band program**. Remember, to establish a championship band program, you entire band should be involved in your program **All Year!**

At the beginning of each grading period have a method to pass out applications for promotions. Make it the individual band member's responsibility to have the application filled out and collect the proper signatures by the deadline. Establish a promotions board to assist you in evaluating each application. In the beginning, you can use your staff, drum majors, or section leaders as your promotions board. As students start to achieve ranks of captain and above, let the high rank members be the promotions board. On the next page, there is an example of a promotions application:

Band Rank Promotion Application

***You may only be promoted one rank at a time—two if you maintain a 4.0.

Name: ____

Current Rank: _____________________ G.P.A: _______

Classification: ___________________

Instrument: _____________________

Reason You Feel That You Should Be Promoted:

Applicant's Signature: ___________________________
Section Leader/Drum Major's Signature: ___________
Grade Level Administrator:________________________
Band Director's Signature: _______________________

Approved _______ Declined _______ New Rank _________

Excellent records must be kept in order to maintain such a program. Keeping up with attendance, grades, discipline, and participation can be time consuming, but the level of student motivation is well worth the time. The last band that I used this program with had an average GPA of 3.2, and an attendance rate of 99%. Students want have standards to shoot for, and like to be recognized for reaching those standards.

National Music Awards

Another alternative to in house awards used for motivation are national music awards. Awards such as the John Philip Sousa Award, Who's Who in Music, or membership in a chapter of Tri-M all can be used to bring recognition to students that achieve high levels of excellence within your program.

Whatever the program you use as motivation, be sure that it is consistent, fair, and brings positive recognition to the individual. Any program that helps with morale within your band is worth the investment.

In conclusion, keeping students motivated is the cornerstone to retention. You must find out what motivates students in your particular community. Be creative and you will see the size of your program grow.

Chapter 9

Organizing Practices and Rehearsals

Practices and rehearsals are the most important aspects of developing a quality band program. It is important to know that there is a difference between "practice" and "rehearsal". Practice is what you do when you are first learning how to do something; be it music or drills or dance routines. Practice should take place at a pace slow enough for everyone to catch on to what is happening. It is an opportunity for students to ask questions, make adjustments, and **make mistakes!** It is where skills are developed and sharpened. All great performances will start with practice.

Rehearsal, on the other hand, is what you do when the practice has been accomplished. It takes place at a faster pace. In rehearsals you go over what you have already learned, working towards perfecting the performance. Many groups never rehearse. They always practice. Therefore the performances are never perfected.

Whether it is practice or rehearsal, there are steps that should be followed in order to be productive every day.

Plan, Plan, Plan

There is an old saying that goes "proper planning prevents poor performance." This statement is extremely true. The reason most bands fail to reach their potential is because of the band director's failure to plan. Rehearsals should be approached the same way as classes are approached: clearly defined objectives and effective planning. "Winging it" leads to chaos, especially with 100 people standing around while you decide what to do. Know each day exactly what you want to get accomplished, and spend every minute of rehearsal accomplishing that objective.

Take advantage of every minute during rehearsal time. Have an exact time to move from one part of rehearsal to another. You will find that you will get a lot more done in a shorter period of time. Here is an example of a time schedule:

Rehearsal—3:00-5:30

3:00-3:15—Take attendance, state objectives for the day, do warm-up exercises (scales, long tones, lip slurs, ect.), pass out new music.

3:15-3:30—Go through previously learned music that will be used for next performance.

3:30-4:10—Go over new music (try to keep it to one new piece a day).

4:10-5:00—(outside rehearsal)—Go over new *section* of show.

5:00-5:20—Add new part of show to previously learned section.

5:20-5:30—Final instructions and dismissal.

This, of course, is just an example. How much time you spend doing each section depends on how far you are in to the marching band season. Keeping to a time schedule requires the band director to have all materials prepared before rehearsal starts, and be prepared to move to the next thing on time. This will keep your rehearsal from being stagnant, and help to keep student morale and motivation up. It leaves very little time to get bored.

Clearly State Your Objectives

Students are more focused and more motivated when they know exactly what will be done in rehearsal each day. If students feel that the band director has no plan for rehearsal, it leads to frustration and boredom.

Know what music you are going to play before rehearsal starts. Write those pieces on the board where everyone can see it. Have your students get in the routine of coming into rehearsal and immediately looking at the board to see what will be played that day. It focuses everyone in on what is about to happen.

When it is time to go outside, take a few minutes while you are still inside to verbally go over what you intend to accomplish outside. Once again, this establishes focus. If there are drill charts to be passed out, pass them out while the band is still seated, and answer any questions before you leave the band room (It is easier for the whole band to listen to directions in the confines of the band room than it is out on a field). Tell the group exactly what position to get in on the field before you go out there.

Establish A Routine

It is much easier to maintain the discipline of the band if there is a well established routine. A set way of rehearsal flow builds stability. Everyone knows what is expected of them, and it is easy to tell who is not in the right place. In order to establish this routine, the band director must be disciplined enough to demand it every day. You must continue to remind the band what the expectations are, and immediately correct anyone that is not following it. Remember, the more routine that you have, the less chaos that you have.

Make Audio and Video Recordings of Rehearsals

Taping your rehearsals allows you to critique your own organizational skills, and how much time is spent on and off task. As a band director, you will become engrossed in what you do. It is easy to miss things that happen during rehearsal that take away from the overall effectiveness of rehearsal. In addition, recording your band allows you to hear your band. You will be surprised at the number of wrong notes, articulations, ect., that are played and are overlooked by the band director. Don't be afraid to allow your band to watch the videos. As a matter of fact, make it a part of your rehearsal time. When students get to see and hear the mistakes they are making, they work hard to fix them. It is also a good habit to tape your performances as a teaching tool as well.

Don't Beat a Dead Horse!

There is a point while practicing a routine, drill, or musical selection that you reach a point of diminishing returns. Learn to know when you have gotten as much out of your band as you are going to get that day. Don't allow effective rehearsal to turn into futility or frustration. When something has been done over and over again and still does not seem to be working, move on to something else, and give yourself time to evaluate your method of teaching that particular thing. Once you have discovered the problem, plan a new way to approach teaching it.

Be Proactive!!!

Do not allow a situation to come up that you do not have a contingency plan for. For example, what do you do if you plan to have an outside rehearsal and 10 minutes before it starts, it starts to rain? You must have a plan in place for such an occasion. For any plan that you have in place, you must plan for "Murphy's Law". Have a back-up plan in place. Be ready to move to your alternate plan immediately when your original plan reaches a snag. Remember, it is important to keep rehearsal moving. Once it comes to a complete stop, it will be hard to get it moving again. Once again, this takes planning.

Always End Rehearsal on a Positive Note

It is good to end rehearsal every day on a positive note. Try to finish each rehearsal doing something that the band does well. Play something they enjoy playing, run through a favorite dance routine, or march through a drill they know well. Many bands end rehearsal by marching back to the band room. The idea here is to make sure that the band leaves rehearsal with their confidence in tact. In addition, make sure that you give them positive feedback. This does not mean don't let them know what they need to work on, but tell them things that you feel they are doing well also.

In Summary, every practice or rehearsal must be planned to take advantage of every minute of rehearsal time. The more time a band director spends planning a rehearsal, the less rehearsal time is required to accomplish the objective. Let your band know what the objective is for each rehearsal. Establish a routine for the flow of rehearsal. This gives students confidence in what must be done. Be proactive. Have an alternate plan for everything that you plan to do. Record your rehearsals and spend time listening and watching the recordings to improve your effectiveness. Learn when your band has reached the point of diminishing returns. Finally, always end rehearsals on a positive note. If you learn to follow these suggestions, you will soon find that you can rehearse for shorter periods of time, and get much more done in that time.

Chapter 10

Preparing for Performances

Performances are the reason that we develop marching bands in the first place. Therefore, it is important to prepare properly for every performance, not only in the rehearsals leading up to performance day, but on the day of a performance. It is important that you establish a routine on performance day. This routine should include the following:

Meeting Time

It is important to have a meeting time established and clearly announced for every performance. This time should be when students should be fully dressed in uniform, have their instruments prepared and put together, and students are in their assigned seats. By establishing this routine you will be prepared to move through your preparations with all members ready to focus on what comes next. There should be a consequence for not being on time, and should be something that will establish the importance of being on time. A good motto to use is "to be on time is to be late, to be early is to be on time." This simply means that in order to be ready at the appropriate time, you must show up early, and not running through the door a minute before it is time to start. Of course, in order for this to work, **you must be the first one there.** Get used to setting a time for yourself that is at least an hour or two before everyone else's report time. Remember, **lead by example!!!!!**

Uniform Inspection

It is important that your band presents itself in the most professional manner every time it performs. This professional showing starts with the proper maintenance and wearing of the uniform. Don't take it for granted that everyone in your band will properly do this. That is why it is important to have a uniform inspection before every performance. This can be done quickly and efficiently if you have strong student leaders in your band. Until you have student leadership, you may want to do it yourself. A proper uniform inspection should include:

1. Cleanliness and sharpness of uniform—All uniforms should be properly cleaned and pressed, and worn properly. There should be no wrinkles in the uniform, all buttons should be in place, and all parts of the uniform are on.
2. Cleanliness of all auxiliary parts of the uniform—This includes gloves, spats, ect. Pay attention to detail, making sure that all members have both gloves, both spats, correct socks, and the correct shoes, cleaned and shined properly.
3. Proper wearing of "under uniform"—This may be a foreign idea to you, but it is important that the band has a specific t-shirt and shorts to wear underneath the outer uniform. This is important in case it becomes necessary for the band or an individual in the band to remove some part of the outer uniform (such as in case of hot weather or illness). You do not want to find out just as you have the band take off the jackets that someone is wearing the wrong shirt!!!!
4. Inappropriate wearing of jewelry or make-up—You should establish a rule for the wearing of makeup and jewelry within the band. Remember, you want everything that band wears to be uniform. Therefore it is a good idea that no make-up or jewelry be worn (with the exception of auxiliary units in some cases).

It is important that an inspection is done before *every* performance. Once again, **pay attention to details!!!** Your band will learn the importance of having everything in place as you continually stress inspections.

Instrument Inspection

Before every performance, it is also important to have an instrument inspection. An instrument inspection consists of making sure that all instruments are in proper playing condition, as well as cleaned and shined. Proper care of instruments insures that performances go over with a lower risk of break-downs. Also, the impression of your band that you leave with the audience depends on not only how you sound, but also how you look. Have a shined instrument add to the professional look of your band. Woodwind sections should take this time to make sure that all players are playing on a good reed and percussionists make sure that everyone has the required sticks. Insist that *all* members adhere to the standards set for cleanliness and equipment needs.

Warm-up and Preparation

Establish a warm-up routine that you use before every performance. This warm-up should include long tones, lip strengthening exercises, scales and chorales. Make sure that your band does not just "go through the motions". During warm-up is when the band should begin to focus on the performance at hand, and should make sure that they are physically and mentally ready. Included in this warm-up period should be a run through of the performance to be done. If it is a half time show, have the band play through the show, while thinking through all of the movements. If your band room is large enough, allow the band to make whatever turns and routines that there are room for. All of this adds to mentally warming up for the show. If you are preparing for a parade, play or sing through each piece of music, so that the band will know how to start and stop each piece that you will play. Have your percussion section play cadences and go through the roll off for each piece.

Having a routine for performance day will make sure that your band is mentally and physically prepared for every performance. Be consistent with your preparations and your standards, and your band members will always present themselves in a professional manner.

Chapter 11

Using and Developing Instrumentation

It will be a very rare occasion when you will take over a band director's position and there is a balanced instrumentation in place, and a middle school feeder program in place that will continually maintain your balance. More often, you will run into the problem of too many percussion or woodwinds, and not enough brass. This situation can be a huge problem, especially the first season that you are the director of that band. However, as a band director, you have to overcome the obvious problems that will come along with unbalanced instrumentation. There are several techniques that you can use to make the best of your instrumentation until you have a chance to correct it:

1. Play music that is written for the instrumentation that you have.

   Too many young band directors make the mistake of attempting to either play music that they got from the college band that they were in, or music written for another more advanced high school band. This is a mistake on several levels. First, the music in most cases is written for much more advanced players (in rhythmic difficulty or in range). Second, the music is written for a band of different instrumentation. The result can be a band that will never hear themselves play as well as they could.

Make sure that the music you choose takes advantage of the instrumentation that you have. For example, if you have three trumpets but seven trombones, choose music that has a melody that the lower brass can play. If you cannot find this music already written, *write it yourself.* No one knows the level of your players better than you. Take the time to learn how to write for your band.

There are some companies, however, that have writers that do an excellent job of writing music for small or instrument challenged bands. To find music that would fit your band, contact publishing companies and ask for their advertisement CD's. In many cases, the CD's will let you hear the full arrangements so that you can hear if it is something that your group can play.

2. Use your woodwind sections to double parts written for brass.

If you have to play music that is written in a range of a section that you have only a few of, support them with another section to help carry the part. For example, if you play a piece that will only sound right if the trumpets play it, but you only have a few trumpets, support them with your clarinets and/or flutes. While these sections can only play so loud, placement on the field and type of reed and mouthpiece can help with this.

3. Combine brass sections to add strength.

In some cases, several brass sections can play together to cover a part. For example, mellophones can be used with baritones or trombones to strengthen a melody. Utilize what you have and experiment to get the sound you want.

It is important that you create the best sound possible from the beginning. Get your band used to hearing themselves play their best. Don't be overly concerned about volume, be concerned about tone quality and intonation. Start from the beginning working on balance and blend. Once you establish a good sound with what you have, start to put in place a plan to build a better instrumentation. If you are going to try to build towards a set instrumentation, it is a good idea to know what a balanced instrumentation should look like. Here are some examples of balanced instrumentation:

<table>
<tr><td>

48 Piece Band

4 Flutes
6 Clarinets
4 Alto saxophones
2 Tenor saxophones
8 Trumpets
4 Mellophones
4 Baritones
6 Trombones
2 Tubas
8 Percussion

</td><td>

64 Piece Band

6 Flutes
8 Clarinets
6 Alto Saxophones
2 Tenor Saxophones
10 Trumpets
6 Mellophones
6 Baritones
8 Trombones
4 Tubas
10 Percussion

</td></tr>
<tr><td>

80 Piece Band

6 Flutes
10 Clarinets
8 Alto Saxophones
2 Tenor Saxophones
12 Trumpets
8 Mellophones
6 Baritones
10 Trombones
6 Tubas
12 Percussion

</td><td>

96 Piece Band

8 Flutes (Piccolos)
10 Clarinets
10 Alto Saxophones
4 Tenor saxophones
16 Trumpets
8 Mellophones
8 Baritones
12 trombones
8 Tubas
12 Percussion

</td></tr>
</table>

128 Piece Band

10 Piccolos
12 Clarinets
12 Alto Saxophones
4 Tenor saxophones
24 Trumpets
12 Mellophones
10 Baritones
16 Trombones
12 Tubas
16 Percussion

There are different methods that can be used to achieve this instrumentation:

1. In-school recruitment

One method of building your instrumentation is by recruiting within the school. In the early spring it could be beneficial to recruit students that may be in general music class or other music classes and begin teaching them the basics on an instrument **that you need to improve your instrumentation.** It is important to steer these students towards the instruments that you need them to play. Adding ten additional drummers when you need brass players is not helping your program.

Starting in early spring allows new students a little time to build an embouchure before the rushed pace of summer and fall marching band begins. It goes without saying, that not all students will be ready to participate at the beginning of summer camp, but every student that is ready improves your instrumentation. Be sure to start them off on the lower parts within sections so that they have time to work towards higher notes.

In some cases, it may be necessary to provide the proper instrument for the student to learn. This is especially true in the case of the larger brass instruments. For methods in acquiring these instruments, see Chapter 6.

2. Middle school recruitment

It should go without saying that your main source for building your instrumentation and your band program should be your middle school band feeder system. This, however is not the case in many instances, and will not be unless some proactive steps are taken. First of all, your will not get your best recruitment if the only time you see the middle school students is when you go over in the spring to try to recruit. It is best to make frequent trips to the middle schools. Offer to assist the middle school director with occasional sectionals, offer your ear as they prepare for concerts, and set up performances in which the high school band and the middle school band can play on the same program. What you want to accomplish is for the middle school students to become familiar with you, and feel that you care about their musical growth. The more they know you care, the more willing they will be to join your high school program. This also allows you many advanced scouting opportunities, getting a chance to find out the skills of each player that will be coming into your program. You will also know what instrumentation to develop within the in-school recruiting and teaching to move towards a balanced instrumentation.

3. Instrument switching

Instrument switching works when your program is very out-of-balance, and changes need to be made from within. Instrument switching does not mean doing away with woodwinds and building an all brass band. It is to make sure that you have strong musicians through your instrumentation. It is best to use students that are already musically strong as those that switch. This cuts down on the amount of time that you will spend in the transfer. A student with a good ear and a strong practice ethic will take it upon themselves to do what is necessary to be a good player on a new instrument.

Once again, it is important when switching students to different instruments that you provide the new instrument. Parents will be much more willing to allow a child to switch to another instrument if it does not require them to purchase a new instrument. Also, assure parents that the instrument that they initially purchased will still be used in a meaningful way by their child (in concert band, jazz band, small ensembles). In some cases the student that switches may actually become stronger on the new instrument than on the original one. That will be even better for your program.

Some instrument switches seem to be more successful that others. Understand that these examples are only opinion, and will not work in every case. Since in most cases, the switch is from woodwind to brass, here are recommended switches.

Original Instrument	New instrument
Flute	Saxophone
Clarinet	Mellophone, Baritone
Saxophone	Trombone, Sousaphone

Another switch that you may want to consider is percussion to brass. Many bands are plagued with way too many drummers for the number of wind players. A way to solve this is by auditioning percussionist and having a set number of percussionists that you are going to use. Once you have selected the players for that number of positions, instead of releasing the others, offer to train them on another instrument. It is possible that you will pick up a few more horn players to help with your instrumentation. It would probably be best when switching a drum player to brass that the switch is made to a brass instrument with a large mouthpiece (i.e. baritone or Sousaphone) to have faster success in producing a sound on the new instrument.

In conclusion, when building a band program it is necessary to use all necessary methods to improve your band's sound and instrumentation. This process begins with developing a strong recruitment program. This starts with recruiting from within your school, while building a strong recruitment program with your feeder schools. While waiting for your recruitment programs to take effect, it may be necessary to switch players from one instrument to another. Make sure that the players that you switch are self-motivated and hard workers, so that the switch will be easier to achieve. Be realistic about what you expect from these players that are switching, so that you don't frustrate them or yourself in the process. Utilizing these three methods will help you build a balanced instrumentation within your program.

Chapter 12

Maintaining and Designing Uniforms

Uniforms are one of the most expensive and time consuming issues faced by a young band director. The ability to inventory, maintain, issue, clean, design, and purchase uniforms can be a huge task. Having a system for each of these issues can save a lot of time and stress.

The first thing a young director will need to do is establish a uniform committee. This committee can be made up of band parents and/or band students. When using either of these groups, be sure that you use trustworthy people that will not play "favorites" when it comes time to issue uniforms. Talk to the band parent president to find out if there is already a committee established. Once you have established a committee, set up a time to meet with them. At this meeting you should give them your guidelines for dealing with uniforms. Also at this meeting, you will want to do a complete uniform inventory of everything that you have on hand. It would also be useful to ask several people on the committee if they know of anyone that may have failed to return their uniform at the end of the previous few years. Uniforms can quickly turn into souvenirs by graduating seniors if a close eye is not kept on inventory. Even if you have enough uniforms the first year, these missing uniforms will become an issue as the band grows.

Maintaining Inventory

As already mentioned, it is very important to maintain an accurate uniform inventory. To do this, you will need to have a standard form that should be filled out by the student, and signed by a parent. This form will allow you to know who is responsible for what uniform, and gives you a signed document to prove it. This form also provides a database of all active band members (it is hard to perform if you don't have a uniform). A good form should contain a space to record all of the following information:

1. Name
2. Address
3. Phone Number (home and cell of parent)
4. Classification (Grade)
5. Instrument
6. Hat
7. Coat
8. Pants
9. Overlay (where applicable)
10. Cape (where applicable)
11. Accessories

It is a good practice to have students purchase and be responsible for things such as gloves and spats, because these things wear out every year and need to be replaced regularly. Therefore, no space on a uniform sheet would be necessary. Also, it is a good idea to issue and take up plumes before and after every performance. This ensures proper storage and upkeep. This data base also comes in handy when small parts to uniforms (or whole uniforms) start to appear with no owners attached.

Computerized database programs are plentiful today, and can make the process of uniform research easier and faster. There are many companies that sell these kinds of programs, and it may be good to get one as soon as possible. When buying new uniforms, insist that the uniform company includes a uniform database with the order.

Take Home vs. School Issue and Take-up

There are several ways to deal with getting your band fitted and into uniforms. The most efficient way is to set up a system where students get fitted and assigned uniforms in classification order, starting from seniors and working down. Students will enjoy this method because it becomes part of the tradition of privilege of moving up in years in the band. For you, it allows the assignment of uniforms to those students that have been fitted for uniforms in the past, and may be able to wear the same uniform. When using this method, it is best to pull all uniforms of students that are returning to the band, so that if higher students need to be fitted for a new uniform, they will not be taking one that already has been adjusted to fit another student.

An important issue to decide before issuing uniforms is whether students will take the uniforms home to keep for the season, or will have to show up early at school before performances to change into uniform, and will have to take them off and leave them at school after each performance. Both of these methods have advantages and disadvantages. Allowing students to take the uniforms home can serve as a great recruitment tool. When students wear their uniforms on the way to school to assemble for a performance, it serves as a human advertisement for the band program. Many parents and future students get to see the pride in which your members wear the uniform close up, instead of at a distance, which is how they usually see them when the band is performing. This can build up interest in the band, and actually increase your recruitment.

Another advantage of students taking uniforms home is that they become responsible for cleaning and maintaining the uniforms. The down side of this practice is that it can become a headache to get all students to turn their uniforms in at the end of the season. It can be a nightmare trying to recover all uniforms by the end of the school year (especially from seniors.) Also, it is possible to lose uniforms during the year as students unexpectedly transfer out of the school. The worse disadvantage of take-home uniforms deals with uniform upkeep. There have been nightmares of students taking uniforms home and failing to hang them up properly, and showing up for a performance in an extremely wrinkled uniform, or worse yet, with iron marks burnt onto the uniform (By the way, wool/polyester blend uniforms should not be ironed.) Also, individual students taking uniforms to the cleaners is an ineffective way of maintaining uniform quality. When a single uniform is sent to the cleaners, it is thrown into the same dirty chemical with all other dirty clothes. You will soon see that the bright colors on the uniform will began to get dull, and other issues on the uniform will start to happen that the cleaners will not be held responsible for. Finally, there have been instances that students fail to get uniforms out of the cleaners in time for a performance.

Having students dress and undress before and after a performance can be an effective process in dealing with uniforms. This is achieved by requiring all students to wear the same kind of t-shirt and shorts to school to wear under the uniforms. A time is assigned for students to pick up uniforms out of the uniform room, and they are required to return them there after the performance is over. The advantage of this method is that your inventory is always at school, and losing parts or whole uniforms will be reduced drastically. Also, you can send uniforms out to the cleaners in bulk, thereby saving money on the cost of uniform cleaning (you can still collect the cost from the students) and being able to negotiate that the uniforms be cleaned in fresh cleaning fluid. You are able to control when the uniforms go to the cleaners and when they come back, therefore you have no issues of students not picking up uniforms from the cleaners in time for performances. Of course, the main disadvantage to this method is time. You will have to allow extra time before and after performances for dressing and undressing. Also, you will have to have uniform committee members be at school early and stay late so that you do not have chaos in the uniform room. This also means more of your time to open and secure the uniform room.

Designing a new uniform

Designing a new show band uniform can be one of the most exciting experiences for a band director. However, if done incorrectly, it can be one of the most frustrating. There are several steps involved in the process of designing a uniform. They are:

1. Coming up with a uniform design
2. Having a sample made
3. Getting a price quote
4. Presentation of the uniform design to the band, school and community

Uniform Design

Coming up with a uniform design requires some thought and consideration. Many school systems require a "uniform committee" be organized to come up with a design that everyone will be happy with. This committee would include you, your staff, a student representative, a parent representative, and a representative from the school administration. Although this idea will get input from many sources, there is an old saying that "a camel is a horse made by committee." It is best that you start with an idea of your own, and present it to the committee for suggestions on how to adjust it.

Uniform Effect

The uniform can play a major factor in the visual effectiveness of a field show. When designing a visually effective uniform three or four colors allow for a variety of color combinations within one uniform. When designing a uniform, think of the words "color shift". Color shift deals with how the use of color accents the movement of the band. For example, if the band is facing the audience, and makes a turn away from them, the uniform should be made to accent this turn. How is this achieved? By using the different colors in the uniform in a variety of combinations on different surfaces. Use of stripes on the pants can work to your advantage or your disadvantage. The stripe on the pants can accent knee lift, or can expose weaknesses in knee lift.

Number of Uniform Parts

Give careful consideration to the number of individual pieces that you have with you uniform. Many bands like to include extra pieces such as citation cords, shoulder blades, sashes, gauntlets, and detachable suspenders. Remember that each of these items raise the cost of the uniform, in some cases, considerably. Also, each of these items adds to extra headache when dealing with inventory and tend to get misplaced, raising upkeep cost. Try to keep the number of parts of your uniform to a minimum, and try to include as many of these effects as a part of the uniform jacket, instead of individual items.

Ease of Uniform Wear

One thing that is often overlooked in designing a uniform is ease of wear. What is meant by this is how easy is it to put on and take off. Keep your uniform as easy to get into and out of as possible, so that your band will be motivated to wear it properly. A uniform that is hard to put on and take off can lead to band members not completely putting it on (leaving jackets or overlays half open, ect.), or students will not be cooperative when it is time to remove the jacket, for instance. You may also want to consider including trousers that can only be worn properly. Bibber pants work well for this. Bibber pants, unlike suspenders, cannot be worn without the straps over the shoulders. They keep the pants up over the waist and at the crotch like they should be worn. They also eliminate a color break in the uniform when a player raises his arms.

Having A Sample Made

Once you have come up with a uniform design that everyone can agree on (good luck!) Your next step is to get a drawing made, and have a sample made. Most uniform companies have computer programs that can quickly put together your ideas. However, if you have someone within your school that can work with you to draw your concept first, it could save you weeks in trying to get a final design on paper. Having a company do your design, unless you are at a site where you can stand there while they do it, can lead to days or weeks of back and forth with you telling them an idea and them sending you their perception of what you said. Sending them a drawing that you have already done gives them a clear idea of what you are thinking. They can then send you a computerized concept picture to approve.

After you have the design on paper, you next want to have a sample made. You want to get samples made by three different companies. The purpose of this is so that your uniform committee can compare the designs of each company, and to compare the quality of construction of each design. This process is of extreme importance before accepting bids, so that you can see the quality that you will be agreeing to and paying for. It is not always best to accept the lowest bid if that company's design and construction is of lesser quality. Inspect the material of each design, as well as the construction of the seams and quality of embroidery of each uniform, and decide which uniforms meet your standards **before** asking for bids.

Getting A Price Quote

Once you have decided which uniform samples meet your standards of quality, your next step is to get a price quote. Price quotes from multiple companies are known as **bids**. Many school systems require you to have at least three bids if they are paying for the uniforms. You want to make sure that the bids that you give them are from three companies whose uniforms have met your quality standards. If you do not have three that meet your standard, keep looking for other companies. Remember, if left to the purchasing department of your school system, they will reward the lowest bidder. It is your responsibility to include only those bids from companies that you could agree with.

Presentation Of The Uniform

Once you have decided on a uniform design, and chosen a uniform company, you will want to set up an opportunity to present the uniform to the band, to the band parents, and to the public. This presentation, if done correctly, can build morale in your band program, help with recruitment, and set the stage for raising the money necessary to purchase them.

An excellent opportunity for this presentation would be during a concert. Advertise in advance that your new uniform will be unveiled at the concert. Make sure that you select a person in your band that the sample uniform will fit the best. Make sure that the student has all necessary accessories (gloves, spats, shoes, ect.), and has excellent posture. Make a lot of fanfare leading up to the moment that the uniform is presented. Take this opportunity to display every part of the uniform, and explain the advantages for each part of it.

If it is necessary to raise money for your uniforms, this is a golden opportunity to kick off your first fundraiser. Have your fundraising committee at this concert, and give them some time to explain to the audience what that first project is. If you are allowed, have several students pass through the audience and collect donations. This could be your first drop in the bucket towards buying your uniforms.

Although the process of purchasing new uniforms can take some time, and can be stressful, try to make it an exciting and enjoyable process for everyone involved, especially yourself!

In summary, uniforms are one of the most expensive items that you will be in charge of as a band director. Make sure that you put in place a plan to deal with every aspect of uniform inventory and upkeep. Establish a uniform committee that can handle issuing and distribution of uniforms. When buying uniforms, carefully consider what will be included in your uniform, and follow all steps in preparing to buy uniforms. If you are careful, you will have a set of uniform that can be used for years to come.

Printed in the USA
CPSIA information can be obtained
at www.ICGtesting.com
JSHW080834170923
48379JS00002B/62